How do they work?

Scooters and Skateboards

Wendy Sadler

Heinemann Library
Chicago, Illinois

Customer Service 888-454-2279
Visit our website at www.heinemannlibrary.com

Editorial: Andrew Farrow and Dan Nunn
Design: Ron Kamen and Dave Oakley/Arnos Design
Picture Research: Hannah Taylor
Production: Duncan Gilbert

Originated by Ambassador Litho Ltd
Printed and bound in China by South China Printing Company.

09 08 07 06 05
10 9 8 7 6 5 4 3 2 1

Library of Congress Cataloging-in-Publication Data
Sadler, Wendy.
  Scooters and skateboards / Wendy Sadler.
    p. cm. -- (How do they work?)
  Includes bibliographical references and index.
  ISBN 1-4034-6827-3 (library bindng-hardcover) -- ISBN 1-4034-6833-8 (pbk.)
  1. Scooters--Juvenile literature. 2. Skateboards--Juvenile literature. I. Title. II. Series.
  TL412.S23 2005
  688.6--dc22
                            2004020541

Acknowledgements
The publishers would like to thank the following for permission to reproduce photographs:
Actionplus (Tim Leighton-Boyce) p. **28**; Buzz Pictures (Mike John) p. **29**; Corbis pp. **10** (Jim Cummins), **21** (Larry Kasperrek/NewSport), **22** (Aaron Chang), **23** (Duomo), **27** (Duomo); Creatas p. **4**; Harcourt Education Ltd (Tudor Photography) pp. **5**, **6**, **7**, **8**, **9**, **12**, **13**, **14**, **15**, **16**, **17**, **18**, **19**, **20**, **24**, **25**; Imagestate (Michael Paras) p. **11**; Stockfile p. **26**.

Cover photograph reproduced with permission of Harcourt Education Ltd (Tudor Photography).

Every effort has been made to contact copyright holders of any material reproduced in this book. Any omissions will be rectified in subsequent printings if notice is given to the publishers.

The paper used to print this book comes from sustainable resources.

Contents

Some words are shown in bold, **like this**. You can find out what they mean by looking in the glossary.

Scooters and Skateboards

This boy is riding a scooter.

handlebar

Scooters and skateboards are toys with wheels. You can use them to move without walking. Scooters have handlebars to help you **balance**.